Perfect roses

THE NATIONAL TRUST

The organic rose watch

The rose is one of the nation's favourite flowers – not only beloved by gardeners, but part of the character of our historic gardens and period homes. Sadly, of all our garden plants, the rose is also one of the most susceptible to pests and diseases and often has a reputation among gardeners as being difficult to manage without the use of chemicals. However, with more and more people turning to greener gardening methods, interest in finding solutions to these problems has now come to the fore. Growing roses organically has many benefits. It is not only better for the environment, but can be cheaper, less work, and – with diverse planting and encouragement of wildlife – it can be more interesting too.

The National Trust has some of the nation's greatest rose gardens and rose collections in its care. It also has an interest in environmentally responsible gardening, but at the same time needs to safeguard the future of its special plants. Choosing new and disease-resistant varieties can help solve pest and disease problems, but is not always an option for the Trust where old-fashioned varieties are needed to reflect the period of a garden or to make a particular historical association.

The National Trust / HDRA organic rose survey

To meet the challenge HDRA, the National Trust and Roses UK have joined forces in an initiative to find effective ways of managing roses organically. Combining the knowledge and experience of amateur and professional gardeners, commercial rose growers and scientists, all aspects of rose care are being covered, but specific attention is given to finding solutions for keeping pests and diseases at bay, especially rose black spot.

The first phase involved gathering and evaluating existing knowledge and experience. The second phase will involve trials testing different management options as well as laboratory trials investigating more novel techniques for controlling diseases. The National Trust will be carrying out informal trials of different management options at various gardens. The information gathered so far is reflected in this book which we hope will give you lots of ideas about how to look after your roses in an environmentally friendly way. To find out more about this project, and how you can get involved, visit the HDRA website www.hdra.org.uk.

Gareth Davies is a Senior Research Officer at HDRA and co-ordinates the Members' Experiment scheme encouraging gardeners to be actively involved in research to develop organic gardening. His work on organic rose management is one of these projects.

A Shropshire Lad

Contents

The National Trust/HDRA organic rose management survey — 3

Roses around the garden — 7
Choosing roses — 11
Formal rose beds — 16
Roses in flower borders — 19
Roses on walls and arches — 20
Roses as ramblers — 22
Roses for hedges — 23
Roses for covering the ground — 24
Roses for small spaces — 26
Roses for wild areas — 27

Where to plant your roses — 29
Site and soil — 30
Improving the soil — 32
Planting roses — 34
Replacing existing roses — 37

Looking after your roses — 39
Feeding — 41
Mulching — 42
Watering — 43
Dead-heading — 44
Pruning — 45
Restoring neglected roses — 49

Avoiding pests and diseases — 51
Common rose diseases — 52
Common rose pests — 55
Plant tonics and non-toxic sprays — 57
Good companions for roses — 58
4 steps to healthy roses — 60

Resources — 63

Roses are worth a place in any garden. The beauty and fragrance of their flowers is unsurpassed. Many varieties give summer-long colour and some go on to produce eye-catching autumn 'hips'.

You don't need a special bed to grow them - there are roses that will fit into flower borders, roses that will climb on walls or scramble over stumps, and even roses that you can grow in pots on the patio.

Many people regard roses as difficult plants – needing heavy feeding, expert pruning and regular spraying with pesticides. However, choose healthy varieties, plant them in the right place and look after them using organic principles, and you too can grow beautiful roses without using chemicals.

Roses around the garden

Roses around the garden

Looking after roses organically means looking after the soil, so that the plants get a good balanced diet. It also means looking after the garden environment – to discourage rose diseases and pests, whilst at the same time encouraging their natural enemies.

Most roses will grow and flower well even if they are not treated with artificial fertilisers and pesticides. However, there are three very common problems that you may encounter:

Black spot – a disease which causes dark irregular blotches on the leaves (see p 52).

Powdery mildew – a disease which causes a powdery white coating on the leaves (see p 53).

Aphids – small clusters of green or pink insects on young shoots (see p 55).

If the roses in your garden suffer from pests or diseases, caring for them organically can help reduce the severity of attacks - often to the point where you can put up with the symptoms, even if they don't disappear completely.

If you are buying new plants, it pays to choose them carefully. Some types and varieties of roses are much more resistant to disease than others.

Buying roses

There are two ways of buying roses:

'Containerised' roses – growing in pots – are available at nurseries and garden centres all year round. This means that if you see a rose that you like in flower, you can buy and plant it straight away. If you plant in spring or summer, regular watering will be essential throughout the season as it will not have had a chance to send out roots into the soil. Check that any containerised rose you buy is firmly rooted and not just a bare-rooted rose that has recently been potted.

Paul's Himalayan Musk

'Bare-rooted' roses - are dug up from the fields at rose nurseries during late autumn and winter. This is a better time for planting because it gives the roots plenty of time to establish before the shoots start to grow. You can order these roses from a catalogue and get them through the post. They are cheaper than containerised roses and there is more choice of varieties. When your roses arrive, don't let the roots dry out. Plant them as soon as possible or, if your site is not prepared, find a temporary place in another part of the garden.

- Check that the roots of any bare-rooted rose that you buy have not started to dry out.

- Check that the plants are healthy and free from disease. All plants should have several healthy sturdy stems.

Choosing the rose you want

You can find types of roses to suit almost any situation in the garden. However, the terms used in catalogues and on garden centre labels can be confusing, and it is easy to be daunted by the sheer number of varieties available. The following pages will help you to choose.

Look out for:

- The height and spread of the plant – roses range from tiny well-behaved miniatures to tall vigorous scramblers.

- The health of the variety – it is essential to choose healthy, vigorous varieties (see page 12) with good resistance to disease. This still gives you plenty of choice!

- Flowering period – some roses flower for much longer periods than others (see page 13).

- The colour, shape and fragrance of the flowers. Many modern as well as traditional varieties have a strong scent.

Finding **healthy varieties**

Some types and varieties of roses are more susceptible than others to the common rose diseases. At one time the choice of healthy roses was very limited – mostly to ones that flowered just for a short time in spring. Now, however, rose breeders are making disease resistance one of their main priorities. This means that you don't have to forego beautiful blooms, fragrance, or a long flowering period to have healthy roses.

To find roses with good disease resistance:

- Look through the following pages; they give some advice on disease resistance.

- Get up-to-date catalogues from the specialist rose nurseries; these are the best places to look for a comprehensive guide.

- Ask the experts; most rose nurseries are happy to give advice.

Disease resistance isn't always easy to pin down. Some rose varieties have become more susceptible to disease with time, and their resistance may also vary with growing conditions and possibly even with where you live - the examples of 'healthy roses' given in this book are only a rough guide.

How long do roses flower for?

'Once-flowering' roses only flower for a few weeks, usually in early to mid summer.

'Repeat flowering roses' flower almost continuously or in several 'flushes' through the summer and into the autumn. Some older varieties flower profusely in early summer, and then have one other flush of flowers late in the season.

Colour, shape and fragrance

You can find roses in soft pastel shades of cream, pink, apricot and purple, in vibrant reds and yellows and in white – almost any colour to suit your taste, although there are no true blue roses. Don't assume that all roses are scented, however – check before you buy. Warmth and moisture in the air bring out the fragrance of roses, so they often smell strongest on still warm evenings or just after a summer rain shower.

Rambling Rector

Tuscany Superb

The roses with the reputation for the richest perfume are the 'old garden roses' grown in the first half of the 19th century. These have loose arching stems and soft cup-shaped flowers - sometimes with intriguing patterns of petals. However many bloom for only a short time and others are prone to disease.

In the 20th century, 'modern roses' brought brighter colours, longer flowering periods, and the elegant pointed rose buds for the florists. Some of them – but not all – are scented. Now you can also get roses which give you the best of both worlds – old world charm and fragrance together with lasting colour and healthy growth.

Old garden roses

- Main height range – 75-180cm
- Health – most once-flowering varieties are relatively trouble-free
- Flowers – many flower only once, but some types are repeat flowering
- Fragrance – many are highly scented
- Colour – mostly soft pinks and crimsons, and white

Examples of healthy fragrant old garden roses are 'Maiden's Blush' (pale pink), 'Jacques Cartier' (rich pink), 'Mme Plantier' (white).

Modern shrub roses

- Main height range – 75-200cm
- Health – many are robust with good disease resistance
- Flowers – nearly all are repeat flowering
- Fragrance – depends on variety
- Colour – whole range

Examples of healthy fragrant modern shrub roses include 'Baby Love' (yellow), 'The Mayflower' (pink), and 'Sophy's Rose' (crimson).

There are many plants which mix well with shrub roses – see page 58.

Formal rose beds

A formal rose bed is the best way to grow what catalogues call 'bush roses' – the 'hybrid tea' roses and 'floribundas'. The stiff upright plants do not generally blend in well with other plants, and they dislike competition at their roots. However, if you give them a plot of their own they can look stunning, and are the best type of rose for cut flowers.

Hybrid teas have large, shapely flowers often borne singly on long stems.

- Main height range – 75-120cm
- Health – depends on variety, recent varieties are likely to be much healthier than early ones
- Flowering period – summer through to early autumn
- Fragrance – many varieties are fragrant although some have no scent
- Colour – wide range

Examples of healthy, fragrant hybrid tea roses include 'Blessings' (pink) - pictured left, 'Icecream' (white), 'Freedom' (yellow), and 'Royal William' (red).

Floribundas have sprays of slightly smaller blooms and give a mass of colour.

- Main height range – 75-120cm
- Health – depends on variety; some recent varieties have good disease resistance
- Flowering period – summer through to early autumn
- Fragrance – sometimes fragrant but older varieties often have no scent
- Colour - whole range

Examples of healthy floribundas include 'Margaret Merrill' (white), 'The Times Rose' (red), 'Sunset Boulevard' (pink), and 'Korresia' (yellow).

Edge rose beds with low growing plants to add interest and attract insects that prey on pests – see page 59.

Examples of healthy floribundas include 'Margaret Merrill' (white) - pictured above, 'The Times Rose' (red), 'Sunset Boulevard' (pink), and 'Korresia' (yellow).

Roses as cut flowers

The bush roses – the hybrid teas and floribundas - with their long stiff stems and shapely blooms are the most popular types of rose for flower arrangements.

For the best blooms:

- on hybrid tea roses, remove the tiny side buds from the main stems and leave the central buds to grow on.

- on floribundas, remove the large young central bud from each truss so that more of the remaining flowers open at the same time.

However, you do not have to do this to enjoy a vase of these roses indoors, and you can cut shorter-stemmed blooms from many modern shrub roses and climbers too.

'Savoy Hotel' (top) and 'Elina (Peaudouce)' both suitable for flower arrangements.

Roses in **flower borders**

Mixing roses with herbaceous plants and annuals in a border is one of the best ways to grow them in a garden. The roses bring a mass of summer colour and fragrance, whilst other plants extend the season and hide any unsightly rose stems. They can also provide food and shelter for natural enemies of the insect pests that attack roses.

'Shrub roses' are the best type of rose for an informal border. This is a very large group of roses that includes all the different types of old garden roses, rugosa shrub roses (see p23) and modern shrub roses, giving you a wide choice.

'Gertrude Jekyll' provides plenty of colour in a mixed flower border.

Roses on **walls** and **arches**

Roses can be trained up walls and fences, on pillars or over arches, allowing you to plant them even in a small garden. Look for a 'climber' not a 'rambler', as climbers have fewer, sturdier stems and often flower for longer. Ramblers are usually more rampant and difficult to train. Shorter less vigorous climbers are best for pillars and for the normal 2 metre high garden walls and fences.

Climbing roses

- Main height range – 2.4-6m
- Health – depends on variety
- Flowering period – most modern varieties flower summer to early autumn
- Fragrance – depends on variety
- Colour – whole range

Examples of healthy fragrant climbers include 'Golden Future' (yellow), 'The Generous Gardener' (pink), 'White Cockade' (white).

Plant a fragrant climber on a warm sheltered wall near a window or door, where you will be able to most appreciate its scent.

'Malvern Hills' (above) ideal for training over arches and trellis.

'The Pilgrim' (right) a suitable climber for walls.

Roses as **ramblers**

Roses described as ramblers are usually very vigorous - the strongest can scramble way up into tall trees. They produce lots of long flexible stems and numerous sprays of small flowers, which can make a stunning display and fill the garden with scent.

If you have an ugly shed or a stark tree stump, or other unsightly object in your garden or on your allotment, a rambling rose could be ideal for covering it. However, check its size before you buy - don't try and contain very vigorous varieties in a small space.

Rambling roses

- Main height range - 3-7.5m
- Health – many have very good disease resistance
- Flowering period – nearly all flower only once
- Fragrance – depends on variety
- Colour - whole range, but pinks and creams predominate.

Examples of healthy, fragrant ramblers include 'Kew Rambler' (pink), 'Adelaide d'Orleans' (white), 'Felicité Perpétue' (pink), and 'The Garland' (pink).

Roses for **hedges**

Some roses can make excellent boundary plants – as a tall scented summer screen, an attractive low divider within the garden, or an impenetrable barrier to keep out unwanted visitors.

The best roses for a boundary hedge are those which: make dense growth, thrive without too much care and are attractive over a long period.

Most 'Rugosa' roses, for example, will grow under poor conditions and make attractive, impenetrable hedges.

Rugosa roses

- Main height range – 90-210cm
- Health – most are free of disease
- Flowering period – intermittently through summer plus autumn hips
- Fragrance – most very fragrant
- Colour – mostly shades of pink, crimson, purple and white

Examples of healthy rugosa roses include 'Roseraie de l'Hay' (crimson/purple), 'Nyveldt's White' (white) and 'Sarah Van Fleet' (pink).

Roses for **covering the ground**

Dense low spreading roses are described as 'ground cover' roses. They could cover open beds or clothe a steep bank, for example. They usually have many clusters of small flowers and provide blooms throughout the summer. Once established, dense ground cover roses will stop weeds from growing. However, before you plant it is essential to get rid of all perennial weeds – those such as dandelions and couch grass that grow from underground roots each year.

Ground cover roses

- Main height range – 45-75cm, spread 1-2m
- Health – some are extremely disease resistant
- Flowers – summer into autumn
- Fragrance – often not scented
- Colour – whole range

Example of healthy ground cover roses include 'Flower Carpet' (white, pink and yellow varieties), 'Grouse' (pink, fragrant), and 'Worcestershire' (yellow).

> *Rugosa roses (left) will grow under poor conditions and make attractive, impenetrable hedges.*
>
> *If it's ground cover that you require, go for dense low spreading roses such as 'Flower Carpet', 'Grouse', 'Worcestershire' or 'Cambridgeshire' (below).*

Roses for **small spaces**

Even if you have a tiny garden, you can still plant roses. Dwarf types such as 'patio' roses provide long-lasting colour in small beds and can even be grown in large pots in a courtyard or on a patio or a balcony. In larger gardens, they can be useful as a neat colourful edging for beds and borders.

Patio roses

- Main height range - 45-60cm
- Health – depends on variety
- Flowers – summer into autumn
- Fragrance – some have a light scent
- Colour – whole range

Examples of healthy patio roses include 'Little Bo Peep' (pink), 'House Beautiful' (yellow), and 'Snowcap' (white). Some of the more compact ground cover roses such as 'Flower Carpet' are also good for growing in small bed and pots.

Molineux (top) and Queen Mother

Roses for **wild areas**

Some roses are suited to more natural areas of the garden. They are more tolerant of poorer conditions and competition from other plants. They also have simple flowers which insects can reach into for nectar and pollen and they have colourful hips which birds can eat in winter.

'Species' roses – the roses found wild in other parts of the world and their near relatives - are particularly suitable. They often make medium-large shrubs with single flowers followed by an attractive show of hips. The Rugosa roses (see page 23) are also good in wild areas.

Species roses

- Main height range -1.2-3m
- Health - robust and mostly disease free
- Flowers – mostly once-flowering, followed by hips
- Fragrance – often not scented
- Colour – whole range

Examples of healthy species roses are *Rosa forrestiana* (crimson), *Rosa oxburgii* (pale pink), and *Rosa primula* (yellow). In a native hedge you could plant the British wild dog rose *Rosa canina*.

action stations

1 **Look around** your garden – there is a place for a rose in almost any garden - whether it is a shrub rose in a border, a climber on a wall, or a small patio rose.

2 **Look for healthy varieties** when you buy – many fine, scented roses now have improved disease resistance too.

3 **Check how big a rose grows** before you buy - make sure it is suited to the space you had in mind.

4 **Check on flowering time**, fragrance and position before buying.

5 **Choose a 'containerised' rose** and plant at any time of the year or a bare root rose from a nursery in the autumn.

2

Where to plant your roses

Site and soil

Roses will keep healthy if you give them the right conditions in which to grow. They like to be cool and moist below ground, and dry, airy and reasonably sunny above ground.

The ideal soil for roses

- is free draining, but not too dry
- is deep and fertile (add plenty of organic matter– see p 32)
- is slightly acidic. You can test this with a pH kit from a garden centre, the best pH for roses is between 6.0-6.9 with 6.5 being ideal.

The ideal site for roses

- is not near large trees or hedges that would compete for food and moisture
- gets at least a few hours of sunshine each day
- is sheltered from strong cold or hot dry winds.

Some roses are more tolerant of less-than-ideal conditions than others. The Rugosa and species roses, for example, will grow in poor soils, vigorous ramblers can be planted near trees, and some climbers such as 'Mme Alfred Carrière' and 'New Dawn' will do well on a shady wall.

Above. New Dawn (left) and Anne Boleyn (right).

Moving a rose

You can move a rose that is in the wrong place. However, if it is more than two or three years old, it will have a large long 'tap' root – which means it will be hard work to dig up and may not re-establish well. Wait until late autumn or winter, cut the stems back to about 15cm above the ground, and dig the plant up with as little damage to the roots as possible. Replant it straight away – don't let the roots dry out. Keep the plant well watered during the following summer.

Improving the soil

Bulky materials such as garden compost, well-rotted manure or other 'soil improvers' bought from garden centres can make most garden soils good for growing roses.

How do soil improvers help?
- they help the soil around the plant roots remain moist
- they help to prevent heavy soils from becoming waterlogged
- they help provide plant nutrients
- they help the plants resist soil-borne diseases.

However, you shouldn't add too much manure or other materials rich in plant foods. Overfeeding the young plants makes them produce lots of lush growth, which is attractive to pests and more prone to disease. On soils which are light and sandy or are heavy to work, top up with 'low nutrient' soil improvers – such as green waste compost which will give the soil a better consistency.

Adding manure and compost to the soil helps preserve the moist conditions roses like below ground.

Soil improvers for roses

- Well-rotted strawy farmyard or stable manure – high in nutrients – allow up to 1 barrow load per 5 square metres of ground (an area two and a half large steps by two large steps) or a bucketful per rose.

- Bagged manures – high in nutrients – add as above.

- Garden compost – usually fairly high in nutrients - allow up to 2. barrowloads per 5 square metres of ground or 2 bucketfuls per rose.

- Green waste compost (made from prunings and other green waste taken to recycling sites) – usually fairly low in nutrients – allow 1-2 barrowloads per 5 square metres of ground or 2-3 bucketfuls per rose.

- Bagged 'soil improvers' – add as for green waste compost.

- Leafmould – low nutrient – add as for green waste compost.

Prepare the whole bed or a generous area (about 1 metre across) for each individual rose. Dig down to about a spade's depth, loosen the soil beneath with a fork. Mix some of your soil improver into the bottom of the hole or trench and mix some with the returning top soil.

Avoid using mushroom compost as it contains lime and can make the soil too alkaline for roses.

Planting roses

When:

Bare-rooted roses – plant late October to mid-March (ideally November)

Containerised roses – can be planted at any time of year

Never plant if the soil is frozen or waterlogged.

How:

Dig a hole that is easily large enough to take the roots. It must be deep enough to allow the base of the stems to be about 3cm below soil level.

- Trim off any weak, diseased or damaged shoots from the plant.
- If you are planting a bare-rooted rose, make sure the hole is wide enough for you to spread out the roots.
- If you are planting a container-grown plant, do not break up the compost around the roots.
- If you are planting a climbing rose against a wall, dig the hole about 45cm away from the wall and slope the plant at an angle towards the wall.

Gradually refill the hole, gently firming down the soil as you do so, and water the plant thoroughly especially if you are planting in spring or summer.

Modern roses are usually 'budded' onto the roots of a wild 'rootstock'. You should be able to see the joint where the stems join the rootstock – the 'bud union'. This should be no more than 3cm below the soil when you plant. If you can't see the join, plant the rose at the same depth as it was in the pot or open ground.

Spacing out plants

Look on the label or in the catalogue to find the planting distance or spread of your roses. In general, be generous with the spacing and make sure that other plants do not overcrowd your roses.

Generous **spacing**

This will allow air to circulate and help to prevent disease. It also makes sure the roses do not have to complete for water and nutrients, and makes mulching and pruning easier.

One exception is roses used for hedging. These should be planted closely together in a row so that, when they are fully grown, the branches intermingle to form a dense screen.

Planting **in pots**

If you are growing dwarf or 'patio' roses in pots and troughs, the plants need plenty of room at their roots and a good potting compost. Choose a pot at least 30-45cm deep with good drainage holes and put a layer of stones or broken polystyrene in the bottom over the drainage holes. Fill with peat-free soil-based potting compost. Plant at the same depth as for roses in the ground.

Replacing existing roses

New roses will not usually thrive if they are planted in ground where existing roses have just been removed. They are said to be affected by 'rose sickness' or 'rose replant disease'. This condition is not fully understood, but is probably caused by harmful organisms in the soil against which new plants have few defences. If you are replacing just one or two roses, you may be able to change the soil around them.

Remove the old roses. Dig out the soil to a depth of 40-45cm over the planting area, and replace it with soil from another part of the garden. Add compost or well-rotted manure – this will add beneficial organisms that can work against the harmful ones.

For larger areas, it is more practical to delay planting:

Take out the old roses. Add compost or well-rotted manure. Grow other plants temporarily – preferably for two or three years. Some gardeners say it helps to grow marigolds (*Tagetes*) during this time.

You can also buy friendly fungi (mycorrhizae) in the form of a powder which you add to the planting hole when you plant new roses. These fungi help the rose roots take up food and water, and make the plants more vigorous and tolerant of disease. Some experience suggests that they can also help in avoiding replant disease.

Remember:

- Choose your site carefully – most roses like to be cool and moist below ground and dry and reasonably sunny above.
- Late autumn is the best time to plant but you can plant containerised roses all year round if conditions are suitable.
- Buy plants with strong healthy stems. Check that the roots of containerised roses fill the pot, and that the roots of bare-rooted roses are not dry.
- Improve the soil with bulky organic materials before planting.

3

Looking after your roses

Looking after your roses

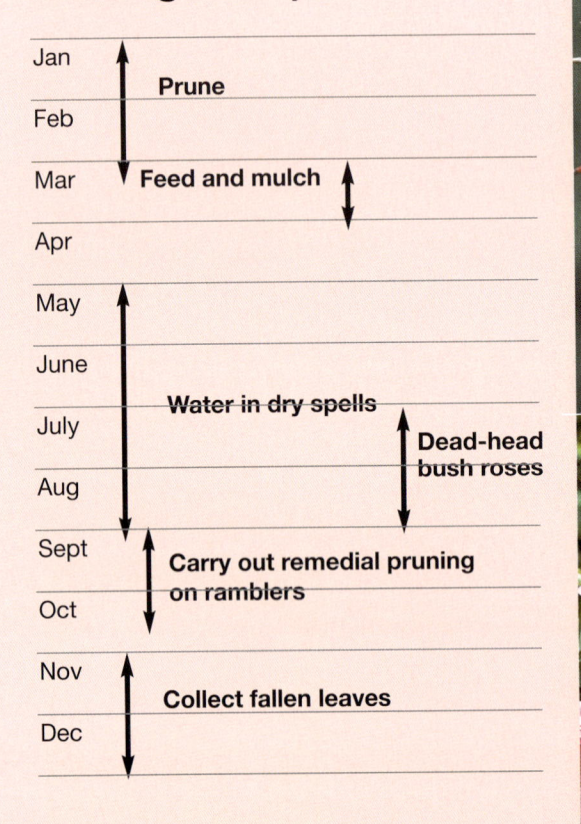

Jan	**Prune**
Feb	
Mar	**Feed and mulch**
Apr	
May	
June	
July	**Water in dry spells**
Aug	**Dead-head bush roses**
Sept	**Carry out remedial pruning on ramblers**
Oct	
Nov	**Collect fallen leaves**
Dec	

Allen Chandler hips (above)
Hyde Hall in full bloom (right).

Feeding roses

Roses put a lot of energy into growing new shoots and flowers every year, and will appreciate being fed - some types more than others. Bush roses, climbing roses and other repeat-flowering roses need most attention.

The best time to feed roses is in early spring, just as you can see their leaf buds start to swell:

- Spread well-rotted farmyard or stable manure containing plenty of straw at the usual rate (see p33) immediately around each plant.

Or

- Spread garden compost at the usual rate (see p33).

Or

- Spread a branded bagged manure at the rate directed on the bag.

Or

- Use a branded general organic fertiliser at the rate directed on the packet. Those which contain at least as much potassium (K) as nitrogen (N) and phosphorus (P) are recommended for roses. Look for the percentages given on the packet. Where possible, buy a product with a recognised organic certification logo.

Too much rich food can be bad for roses. Fertilisers which contain a lot of nitrogen will produce lush growth that is prone to disease.

Mulching

Mulching is an essential part of rose care. Use straw or leafmould, bought-in bark, composted woodchips, or green waste compost, or any other low nutrient material from a sustainable source (such as grass clippings. Spread it in a layer 7-10cm thick so that it completely covers the ground between the plants. It will help to keep the rose roots cool and moist, and to keep down weeds.

The best time to put down the mulch is in early spring, after you have pruned and fed your roses and before they start to come into leaf.
By covering up any of last year's fallen leaves or twigs that might carry disease, the mulch should help prevent the re-infection of new shoots in spring.

By the next winter, some of the mulch will have disappeared into the soil, adding bulk and nutrients.

Watering

In hot dry spells give your roses a really good soaking. This is especially important for:

- Newly planted roses – make sure the soil at the roots is kept moist.
- Repeat-flowering roses – give each a large watering can full (about 9 litres) every week.
- Climbers planted against a wall or fence, as the soil here will usually be very dry – give each a large can and a half every week (about 14 litres).

Use a watering can or a hose pipe, or a 'seep', 'trickle' or 'soaker' hose which leaks water onto the ground at the base of the plants.

Don't use a sprinkler for watering roses, as wetting the leaves can encourage some rose diseases.

Roses in pots need extra feeding and watering. After the first year, top the surface of the pot with a rich compost, bagged manure, or organic fertiliser in spring and then again in July. In between, feed once or twice with a proprietary organic liquid feed, following the instruction on the bottle. Never let the soil dry out.

Dead-heading

Removing the faded flowers from your roses can be an enjoyable job on a warm summer day. It tidies up the plant but is not always necessary.

- Dead-head repeat-flowering roses – it boosts them into flowering again. Snip off the whole flower truss a few inches down the stem once all the flowers on it have faded. The rose can then put all its energy into producing more flowers.
- You don't need to dead-head once-flowering roses. Unless you think they look untidy, leave them on to discourage soft new growth and help prepare the plant for winter.
- Don't remove the flowers if the rose is being grown for its attractive hips.

The winter clean up

- Where practical, collect up rose leaves when they fall and put them on the compost heap.
- When you have pruned your roses, make sure you take away all the prunings.
- Remove any green leaves still left on the plants.

Many of the worst rose diseases overwinter on old leaves and stems. Cleaning up debris from the rose bed can help keep your plants healthy.

Pruning roses

Pruning helps roses produce strong healthy new growth with more flowers, and it can also help prevent the spread of disease. The best time to prune roses in most areas of the UK is during January or February. Wait for mild spells - never prune when it is frosty. In very cold areas, wait until spring growth has just begun.

Successful pruning: Cut out any dead, sickly or weak shoots. Cut back to a healthy stem or to the base of the plant. Cut out any stems of established plants that are old and woody and have not flowered well. Cut them back to the base of the plant to allow new ones to replace them. This keeps the plant vigorous, and stops it becoming overcrowded and prone to disease.

Pruning roses is very easy, and some types of roses need very little pruning at all.

The best time to prune roses is usually in January or February.

Pruning bush and **shrub** roses

For repeat-flowering bush or shrub roses, follow the Successful pruning tips on the previous page, then reduce the height of the whole bush or shrub by a third to a half. You will be cutting the tallest shoots half way along their length, but you may not be cutting the shortest ones at all.

Once-flowering shrub roses should be treated more lightly. After following the first two steps, you may not need to do any more pruning. However, if the plant needs trimming into shape, cut back long straggly shoots by no more than a third.

Training and **pruning ramblers**

Ideally ramblers should be growing in places where they can be left to scramble, with no need for regular pruning to keep them in check. Less vigorous ramblers, however, can be treated like climbers and constrained on pillars and arches by cutting back side shoots to a main framework.

Vigorous ramblers usually produce lots of strong flexible new shoots from the base, which will eventually result in a tangled mass of stems. To thin out and rejuvenate the plant, cut some of the old main stems that have just flowered back to the base and leave the new stems. Early autumn is the best time to do this, whilst the new stems are still pliable.

Removing dead wood helps encourage vigorous, healthy new growth.

Roses pruned, then mulched in early spring.

Training and **pruning climbers**

Attach the main stems of climbing roses to your wall or fence as they grow. Tie them to nails or to a series of horizontal wires.

Train the stems to form a fan-shaped framework, so that they grow more sideways than straight upwards.

Treat long side shoots as main shoots, tying them in to cover the space.

Prune by cutting short side shoots back to about 10-15cm from the main stem.

Attach main stems of climbing roses to your wall or fence; tie them to nails or horizontal wires. Train stems in a fan shape.

Restoring neglected roses

If you have inherited old or neglected roses, the following programme may give them a new lease of life.

- Cut out dead and diseased wood. Cut back to healthy stems, or to the base of the plant if necessary. You will probably need loppers to do this.
- Make sure other plants are not overcrowding the roses. They need plenty of light and air.
- In late winter, cut out some of the old woody stems back to the base of the plant. You can take out up to one quarter of the stems of one plant in any one year.
- In spring, feed the plants with manure, compost or an fertiliser suitable for organic roses (see p41).
- In late spring, put down a thick mulch (see p42).
- Keep the plants well-watered during dry spells in summer.
- Try spraying with seaweed extract or other 'plant tonic' according to the manufacturer's instructions (see p57).

If the roses do not start to grow vigorously and flower well, however, it is better to replace them. Bear in mind that the useful lifetime of many bush and shrub roses can be relatively short (around 15 years) – particularly if they have been either neglected or very heavily pruned each year. Ramblers and species roses, on the other hand, can live for decades.

Replace sickly plants that are a reservoir of disease. There are many healthy and beautiful varieties to choose from!

action stations

1 **Feed roses in early spring** and put down a thick mulch to restrict weeds and retain moisture.

2 **Prune most roses in January or February**, avoiding frosty periods.

3 **Follow the pruning instructions** on page 45, cutting out dead wood and allowing new stems to prosper.

4 **Water** all roses thoroughly in dry spells in summer.

5 **Clear up** fallen leaves and prunings as thoroughly as you can.

4

Avoiding pests and diseases

Common rose **diseases**

Black spot

Symptoms Black/brown blotches on the leaves, which in bad attacks turn yellow and drop. Very common, especially towards the end of summer and in warm damp weather. The disease survives the winter on stems, buds and fallen leaves.

Action Do not plant susceptible varieties. Make sure the site has good air circulation and is not overshadowed by trees. Clear up fallen leaves as thoroughly as possible. Mulch in spring to cover any infected leaves that you missed. Don't use sprinklers for watering. A little black spot towards the end of summer is nothing to worry about (so long as you continue to pick up infected leaves from the ground).

Downy mildew

Symptoms Purplish-red to dark down spots on leaves. The spots differ from black spot in that they have a clearly defined edge, often terminating at a vein. Downy mildew is more likely to occur in lower temperatures early in the year, and is worse in wet weather. The disease survives the winter on stems and fallen leaves.

Action Make sure the site has good air circulation. Clear up fallen leaves and mulch in spring. Avoid using sprinklers.

Powdery mildew

Symptoms Powdery coating on young leaves, spreading to stems and buds. Common especially when roses are planted in dry soil – climbers against hot sunny walls are particularly susceptible. The disease mostly survives the winter in stems and buds.

Action Do not plant susceptible varieties. Make sure the site has good air circulation. Plant climbing roses well away from the wall. Keep plants well watered, and mulch to keep in moisture. Cut out severely affected shoots. The disease should not cause long-term damage to your plants.

Black spot (top) and powdery mildew (below).

Canker and die back

Symptoms A canker is a distinct brown cracked area on the stem. It gradually extends further round the stem and when it encircles it, the whole shoot above it will go brown and die back. Pruned or damaged stems also often die back from the point of damage to where a new shoot emerges.

Action Cut out all cankered stems and dead stumps promptly. Shred and compost them or put them in your 'green waste' bin. If you keep your roses growing well, you don't need to worry unduly about the small lengths of die back from pruning cuts.

Rust

Symptoms Tiny orange swellings on the underside of leaves in summer, especially in mild, wet weather. The disease mostly survives the winter on fallen leaves.

Action Do not plant susceptible varieties. Make sure the site has good air circulation and is not overshadowed by trees. Clear up fallen leaves and mulch in spring. Don't use sprinklers for watering.

Look for Rust on the underside of leaves in mild, wet weather - clearing up fallen leaves in autumn will help reduce outbreaks.

Common rose **pests**

Aphids (greenfly) These are the commonest rose pest – clusters of tiny brownish pink or green insects covering young shoots and buds in spring and early summer.

Short term action Don't panic – healthy roses can usually withstand attacks, and before you know it the natural enemies of aphids will have moved in and have them under control. Meanwhile you can reduce their numbers by squashing the colonies gently by hand, or knocking them off with a jet of water (do this in early morning so the leaves dry quickly). On young roses and for severe attacks which could weaken the plants, spray the affected shoots with a soap or oil-based spray (see p57).

Long term action Don't overfeed your roses as this can cause the soft growth which the aphids prefer. Grow plants nearby which attract beneficial insects (see p59), and make sure your garden is a good home for other aphid predators such as blue tits.

Ladybird adults and larvae both feed voraciously on aphids.

Leaf-eating insects

A whole host of different insects may take a nibble at rose leaves during the summer. These include:

Rose slugworm which eats away at the leaf surface exposing a skeleton of veins.

Leaf cutter bees which cut regular half-moon shaped holes from the edges of the leaves and carry them away to their nest.

Caterpillars and **capsid bugs** both of which eat away at the leaves leaving tattered holes.

Short term action Don't panic – although this seems like a veritable army of pests, **they rarely do any serious damage**. They will not usually affect the health of the plant or the beauty of the flowers. Pick off caterpillars or capsid bugs if you catch them red-handed, but otherwise do nothing.

Long-term action Make sure your garden is a good home for all sorts of wildlife – then you will get a balance between the 'friends' and the 'foes'. The garden should have lots of different flowers, shrubs and trees, grassy areas, nooks and crannies, and ideally a pond. Then it is unlikely that the minor pests which eat rose leaves will get out of hand.

Many ways of encouraging wildlife into the garden are described in the book *Control Pests* in the *Green Essentials* series.

Don't panic! Leaf cutter bees rarely do any serious damage.

Plant **tonics** and **non-toxic sprays**

Sometimes you may feel your roses need a little extra help to stay healthy. 'Plant tonics' including seaweed and other plant extracts are sold with the aim of promoting healthier growth and boosting a plant's natural defences.

As a last resort, there are also 'organically acceptable' sprays – these include formulations of sulphur for use against black spot and powdery mildew on roses, and sprays based on plant oils or fatty acids (soaps) for use against aphids. Remember, all sprays will have some negative impact on insect life and potentially on the environment so use with great care and only when you feel you have to.

If you do buy one of these products, choose a certified product with a recognised organic logo such as that of the HDRA or the Soil Association.

Good **companions** for roses

Putting other plants amongst the roses can enhance a rose bed and may help slow the spread of disease, simply by acting as a physical barrier. In summer, the flowers of these companions can provide nectar and pollen for beneficial insects – hoverflies and lacewings whose larvae feed on aphids, for example, and parasitic wasps that attack caterpillars. In winter, their foliage can provide a dry home for ladybirds and other predators of rose pests. In formal rose beds of hybrid tea and floribunda roses, you can still use other plants as edging around the outside of the beds without spoiling the effect of the display.

Ask your garden centre or nursery for specific advice on which plants to choose as companions for your roses.

Some flowers to grow to **attract pest eating insects**

Hoverflies, small parasitic wasps, lacewings, ladybirds and ladybird larvae are some of the insect predators that will help control pests - attract them by planting some of the following near your roses:

- Cornflower
- Garlic
- Corn marigold
- Sunflower
- Fennel
- Nemophila
- Californian poppy
- Poached egg plant
- Pot marigold
- Annual convolvulus
- French marigolds
- Yarrow

Four steps to **healthy roses**

Roses have a reputation for being prone to pests and diseases but if you grow the right roses in the right place and follow simple rules, you should not need chemical sprays.

1. Roses vary in their susceptibility to disease. If you are buying new roses, choose ones that are vigorous and have good resistance to disease (see p12) and make sure that you choose a good place for them (see 30).

2. Just like us, roses stand the best chance of staying healthy if they are well cared for (see pp 40-47). To minimise disease: never overfeed, mulch at the base and water the roots not the leaves. If any roses are looking sickly, you may be able to restore them by pruning, feeding, mulching and watering (see p49).

Follow the four steps and you too could soon be enjoying beautiful, fragrant and colourful roses such as 'Golden Celebration' (left) and 'Gertrude Jekyl' (this page).

3. Make sure there are other flowers near your roses to attract beneficial insects that prey on pests (see p59).
4. Don't panic if your roses show signs of pests or disease. Check the symptoms with those described in the preceeding pages. They may be nothing to worry about, or, simply caring for the plants properly may help. A few blemishes on the leaves won't harm the plant or stop you enjoying the flowers.

Want more organic gardening help?

Then join HDRA, the national charity for organic gardening, farming and food.

As a member of HDRA you'll gain-
- free access to our Gardening Advisory Service
- access to our three gardens in Warwickshire, Kent and Essex and to 10 more gardens around the UK
- opportunities to attend courses and talks or visit other gardens on Organic Gardens Open Weekends
- discounts when ordering from the Organic Gardening Catalogue
- discounted membership of the Heritage Seed Library
- quarterly magazines full of useful information

You'll also be supporting-
- the conservation of heritage seeds
- an overseas organic advisory service to help small-scale farmers in the tropics
- Duchy Originals HDRA Organic Gardens for Schools
- HDRA Organic Food For All campaign
- research into organic agriculture

To join HDRA ring: 024 7630 3517
email: enquiries@hdra.org.uk
or visit our website: www.hdra.org.uk

Charity No. 298104

HDRA
the organic organisation

Resources

ORGANISATIONS:

HDRA the organic organisation promoting organic gardening farming and food
www.hdra.org.uk
024 7630 3517

Soil Association the heart of organic food and farming
www.soilassociation.org
0117 929 0661

National Trust
0870 458 4000
www.nationaltrust.org.uk

GROWERS:

David Austin Roses Ltd
01902 376300
www.davidaustinroses.com

Find that Rose
From Roses UK and Royal National Rose Society lists all commercially available rose varieties and where to get them:
01727 850461
www.rnrs.org/find_that_rose.html

Pocock's Roses
Tel:01794 367500
www.pococksroses.co.uk

Roses UK
01328 851950
www.rosesuk.com/
– Sources of Rose Varieties

Warners' Roses
01952 604217
email: warners.roses@virgin.net

The Organic Gardening Catalogue
Organic seeds, composts, raised beds, barriers, traps and other organic gardening sundries. All purchases help to fund the HDRA's charity work.
www.organiccatalogue.com
0845 1301304

HDRA Factsheets

Aphids-General,
Factsheet No. PC10, (1997), 2pp.

Biological Control Suppliers, Factsheet No. GG6, (2001), 2pp.

Lacewings,
Factsheet No. GG13, (1993), 2pp.

Ladybirds,
Factsheet GG12, (1993), 3pp.

Mulches: Weed Prevention and Control, Factsheet No.WC2, (2001), 2pp.

Rose Blackspot,
Fact Sheet No. DC7, (1997), 2pp.

Rose Powdery Mildew,
Factsheet DC12, (1999), 2pp.

who, what, where, when and why organic?

for all the answers and tempting offers go to www.whyorganic.org

- Mouthwatering offers on organic produce
- Organic places to shop and stay across the UK
- Seasonal recipes from celebrity chefs
- Expert advice on your food and health
- Soil Association food club – join for just £1 a month

Soil Association
the heart of organic food & farming